*To my dear parents So Hing Bun and Ho Sook Chun,
my lovely wife Mabel Leung and my friends in China,
especially Li Yifu and his family – S.S.*

C is for China copyright © Frances Lincoln Limited 1997
Text and photographs copyright © Sungwan So 1997

First published in Great Britain in 1997 by
Frances Lincoln Limited, 4 Torriano Mews
Torriano Avenue, London NW5 2RZ

First published in 1998 in the United States by
Silver Press
A Division of Simon & Schuster
299 Jefferson Road, Parsippany, NJ 07054

Library of Congress Cataloging-in-Publication Data
So, Sungwan.
C is for China/by Sungwan So.
p. cm.
Originally published: London: Frances Lincoln, 1997.
Summary: An alphabetical and photographic journey through China,
depicting its people, customs, history, religion, and beliefs.
1. China—Juvenile Literature. [1. China.] I. Title
DS706.S6 1997   96-36974
951—dc21   CIP
                                              AC
ISBN 0-382-39785-1 (LSB) 10 9 8 7 6 5 4 3 2 1
ISBN 0-382-39786-X (PBK) 10 9 8 7 6 5 4 3 2 1

Set in 15/20pt Palatino

Printed and bound in Hong Kong

1 3 5 7 9 8 6 4 2

The publishers would like to acknowledge
Mabel Leung as co-writer of the text

C is for CHINA

Sungwan So

SILVER PRESS
Parsippany, New Jersey

Author's note

China is one of the largest countries in the world, almost as big as the whole of Europe, and one quarter of the world's population is Chinese. Modern China has developed from an ancient civilization and features of ancient China are evident in today's art, architecture, and society.

My family come from Guangdong province in southern China. These photographs were taken there, as well as in Guangxi, Yunnan, and Shanxi. It is impossible to show the entire breadth of this vast country, but I have tried to illustrate the common beliefs held by Chinese people and some of their customs, both ancient and modern: their commitment to hard work; their strong sense of family, history, and religion; and their optimism about the future. Images of cities and the countryside show the rich diversity of lifestyles and landscapes, but these are just a taste of what China has to offer. I hope this book will inspire you to visit and explore our country—you are welcome anytime!

算盤

Aa

is for Abacus, a calculating frame with beads which slide on thin rods. The top two beads each equal five, and the lower five each equal one. Even though electronic calculators are becoming popular, many people still prefer to use an abacus—it can be just as fast.

自行车

 **Bb** is for Bicycle, the most common way to travel. China has been called "The Kingdom of Bicycles" because, whatever the weather, we cycle to school and to work, to the market and shops, and from one village to another. As we cycle through crowds and traffic, we ring our bicycle bells to warn pedestrians, other cyclists and drivers that we are coming.

Cc is for China, one of the largest countries in the world. Riverboats are used to transport people and carry goods across the country. The longest rivers are the Yellow River and the Yangtze River, which flow for thousands of miles from west to east, and the Li River which is renowned for its stunning beauty.

中国

Dd is for Dragon, a legendary animal, which is a symbol of strength and luck. With antelope horns, a snakelike body covered in fish scales, and bird-shaped feet, dragons flew through the sky and swam across oceans. The symbol of the dragon is often found in palaces, temples, and as decorations in people's homes.

龙

煅
鍊

 **Ee** is for Exercise. Chinese people practice a body exercise called tai ji (tai chi). It is a sequence of very slow, circular movements and controlled breathing. Tai ji (tai chi) is practiced in the early morning, in outdoor spaces.

Ff

风筝

is for Fengzheng, a Chinese kite. Fengzheng flying is popular and we like to make our own with paper and string. The shapes of a butterfly or bird are common, although sometimes fengzheng are shaped like dragons, caterpillars, and other creatures.

花园

Gg

is for Garden. Many gardens which were owned by wealthy families hundreds of years ago, are public parks today. Pagodas, ornamental structures shaped like temples, were built in the parks, and words describing the beautiful scenery are inscribed on them.

草药

Hh is for Herbal medicine, made from the roots, stems, and leaves of plants. According to ancient legends, Shennong, the god of farmers, tasted all kinds of plants and recorded the medicinal use of them. For many years these plants were gathered from the mountains, but nowadays people grow them. They are then sold in markets or in traditional herbal medicine shops.

Ii

is for Incense, a mixture of aromatic spices burned as an offering to gods, heroes, and ancestors, either at home or in a temple. On the birthday of Confucius, the ancient Chinese philosopher, teachers bring children to his temple, where they light a fire and burn joss sticks and paper money as an offering.

J j 玉

is for Jade, a precious stone which can be different shades of green, yellow or red. It is cut and shaped into bracelets or pendants which are worn from an early age, as we believe that jade protects us from evil spirits.

厨房

Kk is for kitchen. There is a Chinese proverb, "Food comes first among all things," and the kitchen is the focal point of each home. Although electrical appliances like rice cookers are common, we still use traditional utensils: a big, flat knife for chopping and a wok to stir-fry vegetables, meat and fish.

Ll

is for Lantern, the traditional lamp in China. It is made of thin paper which wraps around a bamboo frame supporting a candle inside. Nowadays electric bulbs have replaced candles. Large, red lanterns are hung outside palaces or temples as decoration. They are also hung at the front doors of houses during times of celebration, such as weddings, birthdays or Chinese New Year.

灯笼

市场

Mm

is for Market. In parts of China, peasants are self-sufficient—they grow and produce their own food. They sell some of their crops and vegetables in the market in order to buy things that they cannot grow or make, like chemical fertilizer.

Nn

is for Noodles, a typical dish eaten plain or with other food. Noodles are made from wheat, rice or corn, and are fried or served in soup. We eat them with chopsticks. Some stories say the explorer, Marco Polo, brought noodles from China to Italy, where they became spaghetti.

面条

老

 **Oo** is for Old. There is a Chinese proverb, "Old folks in your family are your treasures." We believe that the elderly have knowledge and experience from which the young can benefit, and we greatly respect them.

图画

Pp is for Picture, drawn in ink-and-wash or *shuimohua*. Different shades of the black ink are created using water. The more water added, the lighter the ink. Color is added to the picture only as a final touch or highlight.

清明

Qq is for Qingming Festival, the day when we pay tribute to our ancestors. We visit our ancestors' graves and clean away weeds and plant flowers. After we kneel to pay our respects, there is a celebration and picnic.

人民币

Rr is for Renminbi, the Chinese currency. Each note, apart from the 100-yuan note, shows the faces of farmers, factory workers, and people from different ethnic groups, to symbolize the union of a country made up of a variety of cultures.

唱歌

Ss is for Singing. Not everybody can read and write in rural China, so they express their feelings, or even pass knowledge on to the next generation, through songs. Some people sing love songs to each other through bamboo "telephones." These are made from two hollow pieces of bamboo joined with string. Sound vibrations from the singing travel along the string.

跳
棋

 **Tt** is for Tiaoqi, a type of chess game using different colored marbles. Each player has ten marbles and the aim of the game is to move them to the opposite corner of the board by jumping across other marbles. The game can be played with up to six people.

Uu

is for Uniform, worn by the police. It is green in summer and brown in winter. On the left sleeve, there is a red star that represents the country, and an emblem of the Great Wall of China which symbolizes the protection offered by the police. They also wear caps and belts, and large snow jackets in winter.

制服

蔬菜

 **Vv** is for Vegetables, an important part of our diet. After the harvest, vegetables are dried in the sun, a cheap way of preserving them. The sun-dried vegetables provide food during the harsh winter months.

Ww

is for Wenzi or Chinese writing.
We use characters, developed from
pictures, each with its own meaning.
Today, Chinese writing in traditional
black ink is considered an art called
calligraphy. We read it from top to
bottom and from right to left.

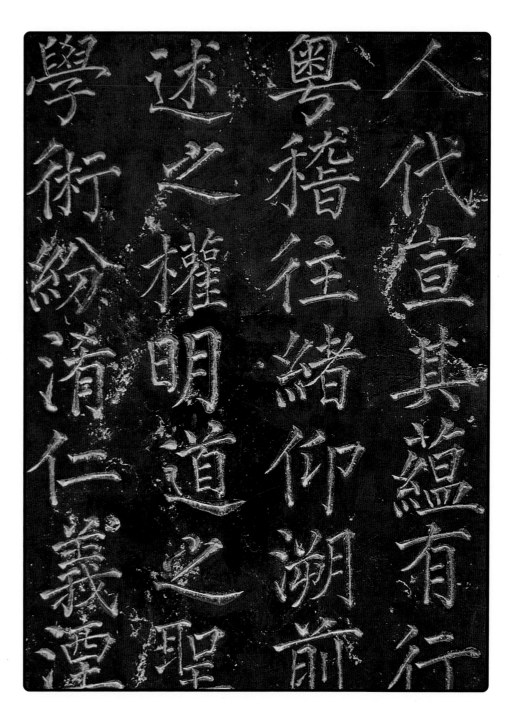

文字

Xx is for Xiao, a musical instrument from ancient times. It is made from a piece of hollow bamboo and is played like a recorder, by blowing through a hole at the top. The player's fingers cover different holes along the length of the bamboo to produce different sounds.

Yy is for Yellow, a color that was worn and used only by the royal family during ancient dynasties. Today yellow is a color for everyone. Schoolchildren wear yellow safety caps so that they can be easily seen on the streets.

Zz

is for Zen, a major religion (commonly known as Chan,) which developed from Buddhism. It teaches inner peace through meditation and enlightenment. The Zen monks shave their hair to symbolize the removal of all the worries of the world. They pray everyday, counting their prayers as beads on the Zen necklace.

禅